MY WORLD OF SCIENCE

Conductors and Insulators

Revised and Updated

Angela Royston

Heinemann
LIBRARY

www.heinemann.co.uk/library
Visit our website to find out more information about Heinemann Library books.

To order:
☎ Phone 44 (0) 1865 888066
📄 Send a fax to 44 (0) 1865 314091
💻 Visit the Heinemann Bookshop at www.heinemann.co.uk/library to browse our catalogue and order online.

First published in Great Britain by Heinemann Library, Halley Court, Jordan Hill, Oxford OX2 8EJ, part of Pearson Education. Heinemann is a registered trademark of Pearson Education Ltd.

Editorial: Diyan Leake
Design: Joanna Hinton-Malivoire
Picture research: Melissa Allison and Mica Brancic
Production: Duncan Gilbert

Originated by Chroma Graphics (Overseas) Pte Ltd
Printed and bound in China by South China Printing Co. Ltd

ISBN 978 0 431 13777 3 (hardback)
12 11 10 09 08
10 9 8 7 6 5 4 3 2 1

ISBN 978 0 431 138350 (paperback)
12 11 10 09 08
10 9 8 7 6 5 4 3 2 1

British Library Cataloguing in Publication Data
Royston, Angela
  Conductors and insulators. – New ed. –
(My world of science)
  1. Electric conductors – Juvenile literature
  2. Electric insulators and insulation – Juvenile literature
  I. Title
  620.1'1297

Acknowledgements
The publishers would like to thank the following for permission to reproduce photographs: © Alamy p. **5** (Blend Images), **11** (Visions of America); © Corbis (RF) p. **15**; © Getty Images p. **17**; © Network Photographers pp. **4**, **28**; © Peter Gould p. **7**; © Photodisc pp. **6**, **29**; © Science Photo Library/ Custom Medical Stock p. **24**; © Trevor Clifford pp. **8**, **9**, **10**, **12**, **13**, **14**, **16**, **18**, **19**, **20**, **21**, **22**, **23**; © Trip pp. **25** (N. Price), **26** (H. Rogers); © Tudor Photography p. **27**.

Cover photograph reproduced with permission of © Getty Images (Image Source Black).

The publishers would like to thank Jon Bliss for his assistance in the preparation of this book.

Every effort has been made to contact copyright holders of any material reproduced in this book. Any omissions will be rectified in subsequent printings if notice is given to the publishers.

Contents

Any words appearing in the text in bold, **like this**, are explained in the glossary.

What is a conductor?

A conductor is something that lets heat or electricity pass through it. A metal spoon may get hot because heat from a hot drink passes along it.

An electric wire conducts electricity.
Electricity passes along the wire from
the plug in the wall and heats up the
metal plate on an iron.

What is an insulator?

An insulator is something that does not let electricity or heat pass through it. Some materials are better insulators than others.

A wooden spoon does not get very hot, because only a small amount of heat passes through it.

Plastic is a good insulator. Each of these wires is covered with plastic. Electricity from the electric wire cannot pass through the plastic.

What is electricity?

Electricity is a force that is used to make things happen. Electricity makes the toaster hot. When the toast is ready, it pops up.

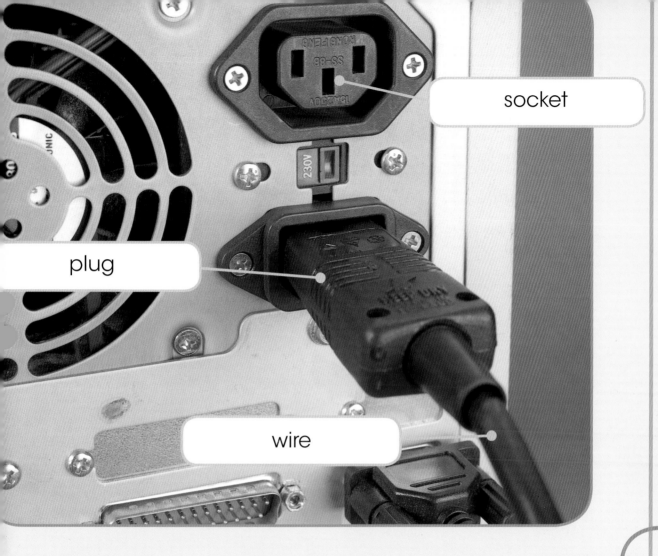

socket

plug

wire

Be safe! Do not touch bare electrical wires or electrical machines that may be hot. Never poke anything into an electric **socket** or electrical machine.

Conducting electricity

An electrical wire is made of thin strands of metal. The wire lets electricity pass from the plug in the wall into an **electrical appliance**.

A television is an electrical appliance.

cable

This train has an **engine** that runs on electricity. The electricity is conducted into the engine from the cable above the train.

A simple circuit

This is a simple **circuit**. The battery stores electricity. Wires conduct electricity from the battery to the bulb and back to the battery. The electricity lights the bulb.

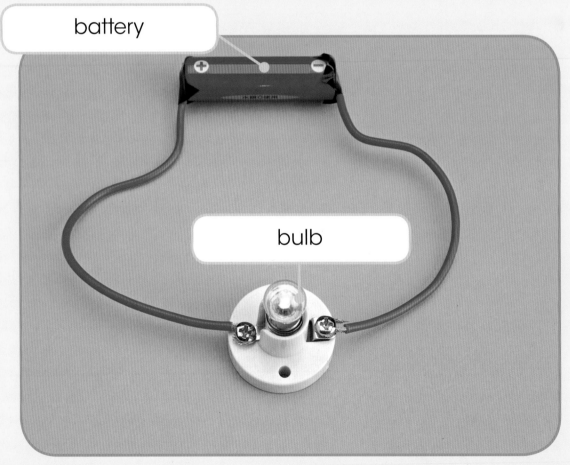

battery

bulb

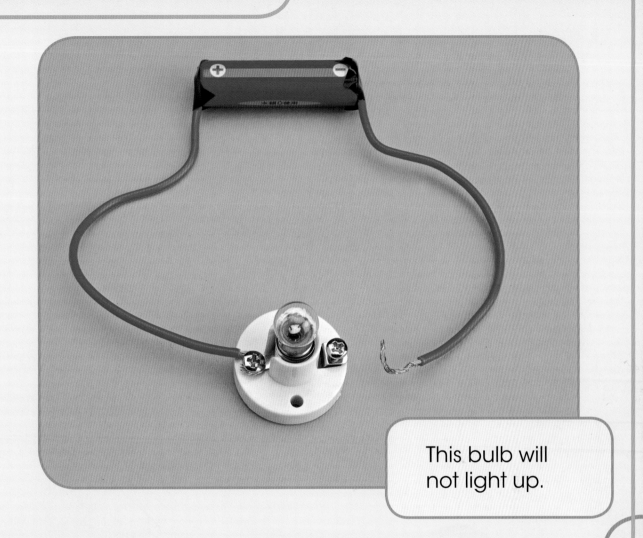

This bulb will not light up.

Electricity will not flow if there is a gap in the circuit. Electricity cannot flow around the circuit in the picture because there is a gap between the wire and the bulb.

Water and electricity

Water conducts electricity. If your hands are wet, water can conduct electricity into your body and give you an **electric shock**.

Make sure your hands are dry before you touch anything electrical.

Never put electrical machines in water. This swimming pool has lights under the water, but they are safe. They have been **sealed** so that the water cannot reach them.

Comparing metals

Some metals conduct electricity better than other metals. **Gold** is a good conductor of electricity.

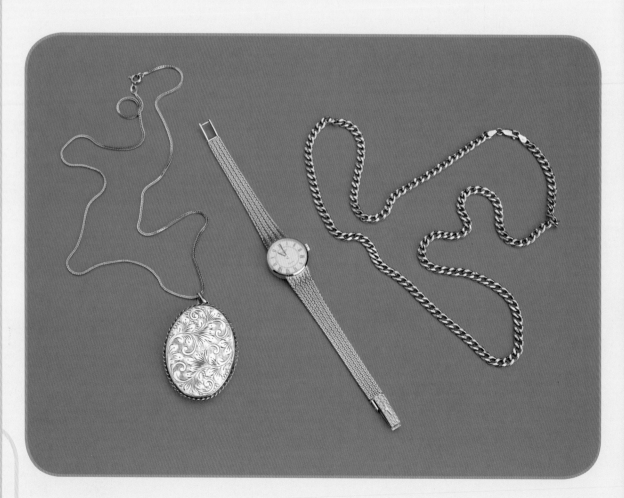

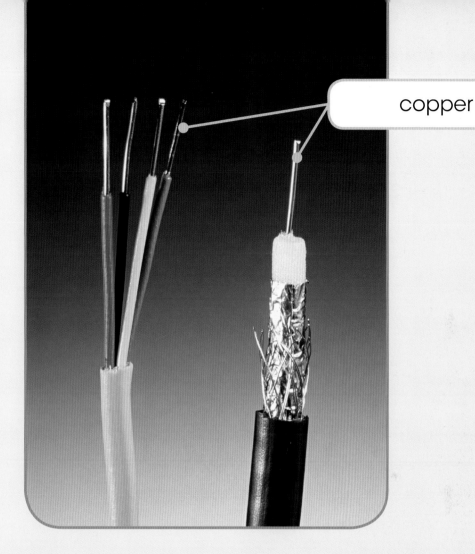

copper

Electric wires and cables are usually made of **copper**. Copper is a good conductor of electricity. It is also much cheaper than gold.

Conducting heat

Most metals conduct heat well. When you touch metal things in summer, the metal feels warm. This is because heat flows from the metal into your skin.

This pan has a layer of **copper** on the bottom. Copper is a good conductor. It spreads heat across the bottom of the pan.

Good insulators

This boy is testing different materials to see whether they are good insulators. When he puts an insulator in the **circuit**, the bulb does not light.

Rubber, cloth, plastic, and wood are good insulators. Now he is testing a leaf in the circuit. Is the leaf a conductor or an insulator? (Answer on page 31.)

Insulating with air

battery

torch

Air can be a good insulator. An electric **circuit** must be complete before electricity can flow. Electricity cannot pass through the air from a battery to a torch.

A thermos flask has one **container** inside another. There is a space with air between the containers. The air stops heat escaping from the inner container.

Clothes

Clothes are good insulators. They keep cold air out and trap warm air near the body.

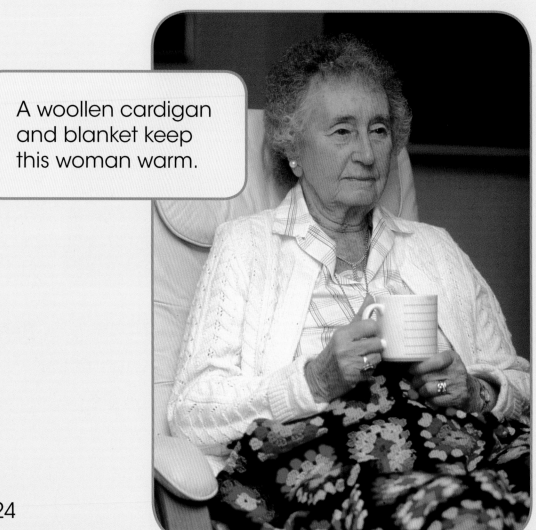

A woollen cardigan and blanket keep this woman warm.

The **fleecy** linings of these coats trap warm air. The children's hats trap air, too. What is keeping their hands warm? (Answer on page 31.)

Other insulators

Wool, cloth, and thick paper do not allow heat to pass through them easily. Thick cardboard boxes keep heat in so that food stays hot.

This coffee is in a special cup that keeps the drink warm. The cup is made of **polystyrene**. Polystyrene is a good insulator.

Using conductors and insulators together

The metal plate under an **iron** gets very hot. The metal plate conducts the heat onto the clothes. The plastic handle insulates the person's hand from the heat.

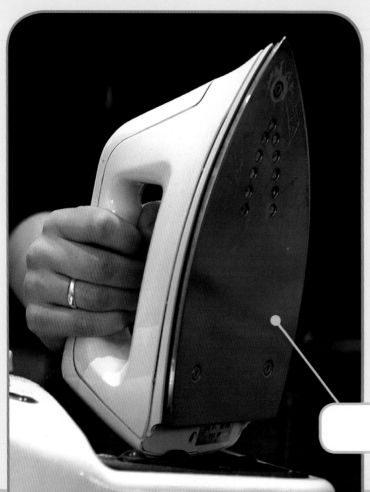

metal plate

This person is taking a hot dish from an oven. She uses oven gloves to insulate her hands so they do not get burnt. What are the oven gloves made of? (Answer on page 31.)

Glossary

circuit   path that allows electricity to flow around it

container   object used to hold something

copper   a kind of metal

electric shock   hard jolt that happens when electricity flows through the body. A powerful electric shock can kill you.

electrical appliance   machine that uses electricity that is used in or around the home

engine   machine that makes something move

fleecy   warm, light, and fluffy

gold   a kind of metal that costs a lot of money

iron   a small, heavy tool that uses heat to make clothes smooth

polystyrene   a kind of plastic that is light and filled with air

seal   close up

socket   hole that an electric plug fits into. The socket joins the plug to electrical wires in the wall.

Answers

Page 21 – The bulb has not lit up. This shows that the leaf is an insulator.

Page 25 – Mittens are keeping the children's hands warm.

Page 29 – The oven gloves are made of thick cloth.

More books to read

Amazing Science: Electricity, Sally Hewitt (Hodder Wayland, 2006)

Discovering Science: Electricity and Magnetism, Rebecca Hunter (Raintree, 2004)

Science in Your Life – Electricity: Turn it on! Wendy Sadler (Raintree, 2005)

Index